D1104165

The Aquinas Lecture, 1976

AQUINAS TO WHITEHEAD: SEVEN CENTURIES OF METAPHYSICS OF RELIGION

Under the auspices of the
Wisconsin-Alpha Chapter of Phi Sigma Tau

By
CHARLES E. HARTSHORNE, Ph.D.

MARQUETTE UNIVERSITY PUBLICATIONS
MILWAUKEE
1976

Library of Congress Catalog Card Number 76-5156

© Copyright 1976
Marquette University

ISBN 0-87462-141-0

Prefatory

The Wisconsin Alpha Chapter of Phi Sigma Tau, the National Honor Society for Philosophy at Marquette University, each year invites a scholar to deliver a lecture in honor of St. Thomas Aquinas. This year the lecture was delivered on Sunday, February 22, 1976.

The 1976 Aquinas Lecture *Aquinas to Whitehead: Seven Centuries of Metaphysics of Religion* was delivered in Todd Wehr Chemistry by Professor Charles E. Hartshorne, Professor of Philosophy, the University of Texas at Austin.

Professor Hartshorne was born on June 5, 1897, in Kittanning, Pennsylvania. He earned the A.B. at Haverford College in 1917, his M.A. at Harvard in 1921 and his Ph.D. in 1923. He studied two years at the University of Freiburg and one year at the University of Marburg in Germany. He began teaching at Harvard University and after three years joined the faculty of the University of Chicago where he taught for the next 27 years, until 1955. He taught at Emory University from 1956 to 1962 and the following year joined the faculty at the University of Texas at Austin, where he became the Ashbel Smith Professor of Philosophy in 1963. Professor Hartshorne has been visiting professor in Germany, India, Australia, and Japan and has given the Terry Lectures (Yale, 1947) and the Dudleian Lectures (Harvard, 1966). He has served as president of the Charles Peirce Society (1950-51), of the American Metaphysical Society (1954-55), and of the Southern Society of Philosophy and Religion (1963-64).

Professor Hartshorne's study has followed two major interests, human knowledge and God. He has sought to advance the process philosophy of Alfred Whitehead. Among his numerous publications are: *The Philosophy and Psychology of Sensation* (1934); *Beyond Humanism* (1937); *Man's Vision of God* (1941); *The Divine Relativity* (1948); *Reality as Social Process* (1953); *Philosophers Speak of God* (1953); *The Logic of Perfection* (1962); *Anselm's Discovery* (1965); *A Natural Theology of Our Time* (1967); *Creative Synthesis and Philosophical*

Method (1970); *Whitehead's Philosophy: Selected Essays, 1935-70* (1972); and articles in many journals.

To these distinguished publications Phi Sigma Tau is pleased to add: *Aquinas to Whitehead: Seven Centuries of Metaphysics of Religion.*

AQUINAS TO WHITEHEAD: SEVEN CENTURIES OF METAPHYSICS OF RELIGION

When I began preparing this lecture I thought I should try to find some way to mitigate the extent of my disagreements with the Thomistic position, seek some almost neutral subject, or perhaps make a comparison of Thomism with my version of process philosophy largely without argument as to which is nearer the truth. However, for better or worse, I hope for better, I have departed from this plan. For one thing it has seemed reasonable to assume that those who selected me for this honor must know my views. To understate these views, to blur issues, would perhaps be an inappropriate way to respond to what seems an act of courage on the part of those who invited me.

The subject of this lecture is too vast

for more than extremely sketchy and selective treatment. However, much of what I shall omit is well known. It is chiefly some rather neglected aspects of intellectual history that I shall be giving you.

I have been called "an anti-Thomistic Thomist." There is this much truth in the description: the Angelic Doctor expressed sharply defined views on some of the chief topics with which I have been concerned. With some, but by no means all, of these views I feel compelled to differ quite definitely. Both the agreements and the disagreements seem more definite than would be suggested by terming me an anti-Hegelian Hegelian—as Marx might be said to be. I do agree with Hegel that the [philosophic] truth is in some sense the "union of contraries" and that, in the subject-object correlation, subject "overlaps." But beyond these vague similarities I find little use for Hegel, whether by way of agreement or disagreement. He seems to be pervasively ambiguous or unclear, and I aim at clarity. So, I think, did the Angelic Doctor.

As Pegis has pointed out, Aquinas wrote chiefly theology rather than philosophy. Here we are concerned with the philosophy that seems more or less clearly implied by, or used in, the theology. Like many other great philosophers and theologians, Aquinas has been very variously estimated. Even among members of the church to whose cause he was dedicated, this has been true.

Long ago in Paris I called upon a pious monk, Père Laberthonnière, who characterized the most influential of thirteenth century thinkers as "the greatest sophist that ever lived." When I asked him to illustrate his meaning, he opened a volume of one of the *Summas* to the place where the problem of evil is dealt with and it is pointed out that God, having the beauty or plenitude of the cosmos in view, endows each creature with its appropriate defects. My French friend's comment was, *"Il s'amuse!"* I thought I understood what he meant. He also declared that he "abhorred the Middle Ages." Like some Protestant scholars, he thought that the influ-

ence of Greek philosophy on theology was
unfortunate. I agree with him and them—
with qualifications.

Gilson once wrote that Saint Thomas
"never doubted" the axioms of his thinking. This is the very reason why philosophers must undertake the task Aquinas
saw no need of, the task of viewing criti-
cally the foundations of what Wolfson has
called "the medieval synthesis." In philosophy no axioms have standing unless and
until the possibility has been seriously con-
sidered that they are at best merely plausible, rather than genuinely self-evident and
certain. We have had too many illustra-
tions of the risks of axiomatic assertion to
dispense with caution at this point. I shall
now give an example of a seemingly self-
evident truth which for two thousand years
escaped critical examination, but which
proved quite vulnerable once it had been
so examined.

In Plato's *Republic*, deity is defined as
"perfect," meaning possessed of a value or
worth so great that no increase or improvement would be conceivable, and no de-

crease either, since the possibility of such corruption would be a defect. (It was taken for granted that change which left the value identical would be meaningless.) In the *Timaeus,* the concept of World Soul (the "moving image of eternity") seems somehow exempt from the foregoing reasoning and to come only as close to unchanging perfection as possible while not quite attaining it.

According to Cornford, the World Soul is Plato's real deity and is to be taken more seriously than the demiurge, the latter being a mythical figure—or a mere abstraction, the rational element in the World Soul. We shall meet something like this idea again in Whitehead. But Aristotle, "first and greatest of the neoplatonists," dropped the World Soul and took divine immutable perfection literally. He was followed in this for two millennia by nearly all theists in the West, and still to this day by some.

Aristotle drew an important consequence from the assumed immutability of deity. A being that could not change can have no unactualized potentiality in its reality; whatever it could be it is. It is pure actuality. Any contingency with respect to it can only mean at most that some effects it might have produced have not occurred. But in itself it is, necessarily, all that it is capable of being. Any relations between deity and contingent events in the world (relations that might have been otherwise, since the events might have been otherwise) will qualify the events but not deity. Had the events and their relations been otherwise, deity would not have been otherwise. Just this is what Aquinas asserts when he says that relations between God and the world are relations for the world but not for God. So far there is agreement with "the [Greek] philosopher." But Aristotle deduces a momentous corollary: since to know something is to be related to it, to really have it as relatum, God cannot know contingent or changeable things. He can know only eternal necessities, he can think only the essence of thinking itself, the form of forms. At this point all Christian and most Islamic and Jewish thinkers (with Gersonides a notable exception) felt it necessary to depart from Aristotle. They could not deny divine omniscience and retain any plausible agreement with Scripture. The question remains, was not the Aristotelian deduction valid? To know is to sustain a genuine relation to the known, a relation that must be contingent if the known is so; hence, a being without internal contingency cannot know contingent things.

The argument is by no means, as it is sometimes accused of being, that every property of the known must be also a property of the knowing and the knower. Quite the contrary, there can be contingent knowledge of the necessary. Had I not existed, my knowledge of some necessary truth, say that two and two are four, would not have been. So this knowledge is contingent, though its object is not. It is the reverse contrast that makes trouble; for if a certain instance of knowledge could not have failed to be, how could its object have failed to be?

We find the great scholastic agreeing

with Aristotle that in all ordinary cases the knower conforms to, depends upon, the known, is in real relation to the latter. However, we are boldly informed, with divine knowing, the case is opposite: here the known depends upon the knowing and the knower. Here the sole genuine relation is in the known. It seems to follow that "God knows the world" is but an inverted and possibly misleading way of saying that the world is known by God.

I have argued against this view in many places. What I want to do here is to stress the following: Aristotle and Thomas are in my opinion splendidly right against much modern thought on two points—there are one-way relations of dependency, and ordinary forms of knowing furnish instances. One can know something because there is that something: when we know a thing we do not thereby bring it into existence; rather, the existence of the thing is a condition of our enjoying this knowledge. Now the very idea of such one-way dependence is flatly contradicted by Hume's famous axiom, "the distinguishable is separable," unless we mean by this, as Hume did not, that of two distinguishable terms, x and y, *at least one* must be capable of existing without the other. *Two-way* separability is not entailed by distinguishability. Not only Hume but many of his admirers down to this day, including the late Bertrand Russell, fail to see the importance of this reservation.

Aristotle and his great medieval admirer are also, I hold, right on a third point. There is a one-way (and thus non-Humean) dependence of worldly things upon God. God could have existed though every detail in the world had been otherwise, but without God nothing could exist. Hume's axiom, taken literally, would mean that either God and his creatures are indistinguishable or the latter could have existed without God. So by a supposedly harmless or self-evident axiom Hume disposed of the basic theistic idea of divine independence as contrasted to creaturely dependence. Why bother to write long discussions of the theistic question if the matter is so simply settled?

Hume was treating as self-evidently false two basic beliefs of most previous philosophy, the idea of the *unique* independence of deity and the idea of the *one-way* dependence of knowing on things known. It is time we stopped letting Hume "get away with" this cavalier procedure. I find admirable the Thomistic discussion of the point that, although the human mind is such that we feel compelled to say of every relation that it has a converse, thus "knowing" and "being known," yet, in normal cases at least, the converse is merely a reverse way of expressing the sole ontological epistemic relation, which is the one actualized in the knowing rather than in the known. To be known is not a real property, or is real only "in the mind." We know Plato; what is that to Plato? It is indeed something to us.

Nothing in the foregoing paragraph justifies the medieval inversion of cognitive dependency in speaking (by analogy) of God's knowledge. The reasons given for this inversion include the considerations: God is the cause of all things, and in knowledge of a cause its effects are known; hence in merely knowing himself God must know whatever things he could produce and needs no further relation to the things. According to the metaphysics that I accept and regard as *the* twentieth-century form of metaphysics (much as scholasticism represented the medieval form), to know a cause adequately is indeed to know its *possible* results. However, causes never imply any precise actual results, but only a range of possible ones. Thus God, merely in knowing his eternal essence, would know "possible worlds" so far as these are eternally implied by the essence; but he would not thereby know the actual world. Causes always leave results somewhat open for further decision. This is the *universal creativity* that current metaphysics (process philosophy) regards as the form of forms.

It may seem that if the knower as such asymmetrically depends upon the known and yet there is one-way dependence of creatures upon God, then Aristotle was right, God cannot know the creatures. We shall see that this does not follow. Something in God may depend upon the creatures without his very existence or eternal essence being thus dependent. God may have accidents as well as essence, and with respect to the latter, but not the former, he may be asymmetrically independent of the actual world.

We now skip to Spinoza. He agreed with Aristotle in the view that knowing implicates the known: hence *if* God is without contingency, then either (1) all things are as necessary as God or (2) God does not know all things. Aristotle has taken the second horn of the dilemma; Spinoza, knowing well how revolutionary his decision was, took the first. (Of course the Stoics had preceded him, but scarcely any medieval writer.) A third possibility remains: admit contingency and change in deity as well as in the world. The Plato of the *Timaeus* could be interpreted as furnishing a precedent for this view, but Plato scarcely made the matter clear. On the whole, to admit divine change had to be a violent break with two thousand years of natural theology.

It was the little noticed heretical Christian sect of Socinians who dared to take this step. (One Arabian thinker had, somewhat ambiguously, preceded them.) The Socinians took human freedom seriously, interpreting this to mean that human decisions, so far as free, cannot be known in advance, since in advance they do not exist to be known. (The apparent solution, the decisions are known not in advance but eternally, out of time altogether, they may or may not have discussed. Some of us think that the solution is only apparent, for if the decisions do not exist in advance, a fortiori they do not exist eternally or out of time. The idea of events spread out for divine contemplation in a finished series, some future to us, is a form of the "spatializing of time," that Bergson has taught some of us to reject.) The Socinians argued: omniscience knows things as they are, the past and definite as such, the future and partly indefinite also as such. To "know" the indefinite as definite is not knowledge but error. Cicero had hinted at

such a view long before, and so had the
Arabian thinker mentioned.

If God acquires new knowledge as new
things are there to be known, the eternity
of God cannot mean his immutability.
"God is eternal," the Socinians said, "in
that he cannot not exist." This implies that
the divine essence (what makes God God
and not a mere creature) is necessarily
actualized somehow, that is, in some states
of knowledge that are omniscient in the
sense defined, yet with contingent aspects
and with significant increments as reality
itself acquires new items. There is in this
knowledge no loss but only gain. Change
is taken not to entail corruptibility. What
a revolution! It was two centuries before
anything closely similar was again pro-
posed. The Socinians are the real forerun-
ners of process theology, and indeed almost of process philosophy generally. For
if even deity is in process, the whole idea
of becoming as an inferior form of being
cannot be sound. Moreover, the Socinians
affirmed not only creaturely and divine
contingency, but also creaturely and di-

vine creativity and freedom (at least for human creatures) in the strong sense of enriching the definiteness of reality. Yet they preserved the necessary asymmetrical dependence of the creatures upon God. No creature, only deity, is such that it "could not not exist."

The entire history of philosophical theology, from Plato to Whitehead, can be focused on the relations among three propositions:

(1) The world is mutable and contingent;

(2) The ground of its possibility is a being unconditionally and in all respects necessary and immutable;

(3) The necessary being, God, has ideally complete knowledge of the world.

Aristotle, Spinoza, Socinus, and process philosophers agree that the three propositions, taken without qualification, form an inconsistent triad, for they imply the contradiction: a wholly non-contingent being has contingent knowledge (since its object might not have existed). Aristotle and a few Jewish or Arabian disciples remove the contradiction by qualifying (3), the divine knowledge; Spinoza and the Stoics remove it by rejecting (1), worldly contingency; Socinus, Fechner, Lequier, and process philosophers remove it by qualifying (2), the immutability and sheer necessity of deity. Thus all three propositions have been deliberately challenged. In each case the challengers knew well what they were questioning. And all agree that the triad is inconsistent.

Proposition (1) can be qualified in a more subtle way than by the outright Stoic rejection. As process theologians hold about God that he is both necessary and contingent, both mutable and immutable, so one may, with Whitehead and Aristotle, hold about the world that it is both necessary and contingent. For, granted that everything particular or specific in the world might have been different, it does not by any logical rule follow necessarily that there might have been no world at all, i.e., that God might have refrained from creating, or might have had no effects. It is one thing for an agent to have freedom to do this or to do that instead; it is another for the agent to have freedom to do nothing. What is the value of the alleged freedom not to act? Is not any world better than none? If so, there is no praise of God in the assertion that he was capable of doing the worst possible thing, i.e., letting his creative power lie completely idle. Whitehead says, in effect, that the mere abstract truth that there is a world, something distinguishable from God, is necessary, not contingent. The existence of the world, some world or other, lies, he says, "beyond the accidents of God's will." God does not choose to have a world, though he does choose to have one with such and such general characters, e.g., such and such natural laws. As for the details of the world, they are not divinely chosen but are acts of creaturely freedom. The Thomistic proposition, "existence is an act," is good process philosophy.

There are nine possible ways of conceiving the modality of God and the world. Using capital letters for divine modalities:

N for divine necessity, C for divine contingency; small letters for worldly modalities: n for worldly necessity, c for worldly contingency, we have, as formal possibilities: NC/nc, NC/n, NC/c; N/nc, N/n, N/c; C/nc, C/n, C/c. Of these nine formally possible doctrines, six are historically important: NC/nc, process philosophy; N/n, Stoicism and Spinoza; N/c, medieval theology; N/nc, Aristotelianism; NC/c, presumably Socinianism and perhaps Jules Lequier; C/c, doctrines of a merely contingent deity, Mill (in some moods at least), William James, and John Hick.

Against N/n there are two objections: (1) It destroys the asymmetry between dependent world and independent deity; for if God necessarily makes just the world that exists, then he is not independent of the world any more than it is independent of him. Yet the whole point of introducing God is the one-sided dependence of things upon him. Moreover, (2) there is the principle of contrast: necessity is significant because there is also contingency. Against N/c there is the argument of Aristotle, also of Spinoza and process philosophy, that N/c makes it impossible to construe the religious idea of divine knowledge. As Maimonides put it, on this basis God has "knowledge" only in the sense in which the dogstar is a dog. There is equivocation. Gersonides took this as a *reductio ad absurdum*. N/c also makes equally unconstruable what is meant by divine freedom. Whatever God is, that he could not fail to be: hence if God is the decider who wills, "let there be such and such a world," he could not have failed to be that very decider. Wherein is the freedom? Against NC/c there is the objection that, like N/c, it attributes to deity an idle capacity not to create at all.

Against C/c there is one of the two objections urged against N/n, that it violates the principle of contrast, and also the objection that if God is wholly contingent then we need an explanation of his existence. The only explanation of the contingent is a genetic one, how it came to be, under what antecedent conditions. But God is conceived as ungenerated, in es-

sence uncaused. It follows that the only
explanation of his existence must be that
of a priori necessity, as in 2 and 2 make 4.
There must be some inconceivability in
the contradictory. This is the point of the
ontological argument, not that it alone suffices to prove the existence of deity (I
agree with Thomas of Aquino that it does
not), but that it shows the inadequacy of
mere empiricism to adjudicate the theistic
question.

In the nineteenth century, philosophers
and theologians in increasing numbers
began to move away from the classical
view that becoming is merely an inferior
form of being. Thus Hegel proclaimed
that mere being, like mere nonbeing, is
empty, and that becoming is the synthesis.
But who knows what happens to contingency and freedom in Hegel? I have tried
to find out but have given up. Hegel uses
the word contingent, but what does he
assert and what deny when he does so?
Let Hegelians answer. I prefer people
whose language is plainer than Hegel's.
Schelling is sometimes clearer, but not

much.

After Hegel at least three writers re-
affirm the Socinian position concerning the
dual modality and partial mutability of
God: these are: Fechner and Pfleiderer in
Germany, and Jules Lequier in France.
Perhaps only the last knew about the Socinians. Fechner and Lequier had some influence on William James, who, however,
failed to do justice to the theological aspects of their work. In my opinion, they
surpassed him as natural theologians.

Early in the present century additional
philosophers and theologians adopted the
view of a deity with both necessary and
contingent, both eternal and temporal, aspects. William P. Montague and E. S.
Brightman were two of these, my teacher
W. E. Hocking was a third. Finally the
great system-maker Whitehead distinguished two aspects of the divine reality,
the one "primordial" and independent of
all particular creatures, the other "consequent" and dependent upon particular
creatures.

The principle that Socinus, Fechner,

Lequier, and the other four just mentioned have in common I call the *principle of dual transcendence*. Instead of distinguishing God from other beings by terming him simply necessary, infinite, independent, eternal, while the others are simply contingent, finite, dependent, temporal, the contrast is made in dual terms: God is, in uniquely excellent ways, *both* necessary and contingent, both infinite and finite, independent and dependent, eternal and temporal. Brightman's phrase "finite-infinite God" illustrates the duality in question. If this scheme is to be shown to be acceptable, it is clearly necessary to meet two objections: one that the duality is really contradiction, and hence logically impossible; and the other that, whereas simple transcendence gave an unambiguous contrast between deity and mere creatures, the dual version blurs and perhaps obliterates the contrast.

The question of contradiction is the easier one to answer. The law of non-contradiction is incorrectly expressed by "no subject can have the predicates p and not-p;" one must add the qualification, "in the same respect." A person can change in some respects without changing in every respect; the world may be finite spatially and infinite temporally. God may be immutable in his ultimate purpose but adopt new specific objectives in response to new acts by the creatures. He may exist necessarily so far as his essence is concerned but contingently so far as inessential qualities are in question. The two aspects are not on the same ontological level; for the essence or ultimate purpose is abstract and the specific aims are concrete. And we can appeal to the Aristotelian principle that the abstract is real in the concrete. God may have infinite potentialities but finite actuality. Potentialities are abstractions, only the actual is concrete. Moreover, it is possibilities that are infinite; actuality is always a decision among possibilities, excluding some from realization. Any possible state of the world would be content of God's knowledge if it were actual, but not even God can contradictorily enjoy all possible world states as actual, for there are mutually incompossible ones. Even the supreme artist must leave something undone. Moreover, his creatures so far as free must do so also, and what they exclude is excluded even for God. God would have had me as doer of some deed I *might* have performed, but since I did not perform it he now can never have that possible me.

The removal of the apparent contradiction in the idea of dual transcendence by distinguishing divine aspects or respects may be rejected on the ground of the divine "simplicity." But this begs the question. Only nondual transcendence supposes that God is the simplest of realities and merely that. Rather he is both the simplest and the most complex, the latter applying to his concrete reality. And the distinction between the abstract and the concrete aspects is the duality we need to remove the contradiction. Only God's essence is simple, not his full reality as including also contingent properties.

Does dual transcendence blur the contrast between God and other realities? I have argued at length that this is not the

case. Any creature has a temporal beginning and termination. God has neither.
His form of temporality excludes birth
and death; it also excludes corruption or
any change consisting in decrease in value.
Only increase is possible for Him. These
are very clear differences indeed. Again
take the infinity of divine potentiality. It
too is unique to God. We creatures are
finite not only in actuality but even in potentiality. We also are contingent not only
in some but in all our qualities; we have
individually, or even as species, no necessary essence that could not fail to exist.
With every pair of contraries it can be
shown that the uniqueness of God is definitely statable in dual terms. For instance,
God, in contrast to us, is dependent upon,
as knower of, not just *some* but *all* worldly
events. Thus his dependence, i.e., sensitiv-
ity or responsiveness, is as truly unique as
his independence, both being with respect
to all events. Similarly, though the contrast
actual-possible applies to God and the
creatures, it applies uniquely to the former
since only *his* actuality includes all actual-

ity, and only his potentiality includes all
potentiality. God may have exhaustive
awareness of what actualities there are;
but, unless he is ready to acquire new
actualities should they be actualized, his
reality cannot measure the importance that
we in practice assume, whatever we may
say, for their actualization. Just as for
things to be actual must mean to be actual
for God, so for them to be possible must
mean to be possible for God. Thus, if we
acquire new knowledge of things already
known to God, as we keep doing in
science, although this removal of our previous ignorance, this self-improvement, is
not such an improvement for God, who is
never ignorant, nevertheless, the new human experiences involved are new data
enjoyed by divine perception, and so God
has new knowledge of new truths, instead
of, as with us, removal of previous ignorance of truths already in being. His knowledge is thus enriched, rather than made
more adequate to its data. Similarly, if
we pass from ethically inferior to ethically superior modes of volition, we do not

thereby ennoble deity, who cannot be ig-
noble. But we present God with a more
beautiful creation than he enjoyed before.
On such matters Fechner was wonderfully
clear long ago, in a world that was too
busy to notice. Fechner beautifully com-
pares the appreciation in God of new human responses to things not new to God
with a human parent's enjoyment of small
children who, each in ways without exact
precedent, respond with the thrill of novelty to features of the world long familiar
to the parent.[1]

I cannot think of a better example than
Fechner's of how true it is that things
worth saying, not previously said, can be
well said without producing much effect,
at least for long periods of time. There is
an element of chance in such things. It is
quite clear that James, if (which I doubt)
he ever read Fechner's long chapter on
"God and the World" in *Zendavesta*, mis-
understood or forgot its message. I say
this because Fechner's view meets James's
basic requirements that there be an open
future for God and that our choices make

a contingent difference to him. So far from
recognizing this common ground James
writes as though Fechner's God were simply one more version of "the absolute" for
whom the future is a closed book.

More recently Berdyaev and Whitehead
are similarly on James's side in what mat-
tered most to him, but not only did James
die too soon to find this out, but also and
more important is the fact that most of
those influenced by James, notably John
Dewey, never permitted themselves to
acknowledge how far theological devel-
opments went, early in this century, to
provide the values that James sought.
Dewey's critique of traditional theism is
largely irrelevant to the work of Berdyaev,
Whitehead, or Dewey's colleague at Barn-
ard College (Columbia), William P. Montague. I once asked Montague if Dewey
had ever adapted his criticisms of theology
to Montague's form of process metaphysics. Montague thought I was correct in
denying this. Dewey writes in *A Common
Faith* as though no such form of theism
existed, indeed as though Socinus, Fech-

ner, Lequier, Whitehead, or any thinkers like them were out of the question. Most writers, especially those whose inspiration is largely British, are still so writing. To quote the late matchless Mortimer Snerd, "That's the way it goes."

There was one important omission in Plato's formula for soul or mind. Mind is as remarkable for its capacity to be moved by others as for its "self-motion." Memory and perception are ways of being influenced, not of influencing. It is objects as such that influence subjects, not vice versa. This is merely the asymmetry referred to in the theory of knower and known. If we think of the cosmic soul (Plato's formula for deity) as moving but unmoved, we think of it as object not as subject. To know is to receive influence. To be known is to exert influence. Every writer should be aware of this. He wants to be known so that he may move others. All the knowing in him you please will not move others unless they become the knowers of this knowing. It is odd that so much of the history of thought seems a denial of these patent truisms.

A curious attempt that I recall from a scholastic treatise to show how the unmoved can move others is the idea of a very strong man who lifts a weight almost without seeming to move himself, whereas a weaker man would exhibit more obvious bodily movements. More obvious but not more genuine or massive! Plenty of change in the muscle tissues, the blood stream, and what not will alone make the weight rise. Such mythical examples are not a good basis for sound thinking. Physical examples which presume physical knowledge that is in fact not to be had, or which contradict the knowledge we do have, are best discarded.

We have been galloping back and forth through seven (or twenty-five) centuries of intellectual development. Of course many questions have been ignored. One of them is this: process philosophy, Socinus to Whitehead, seems to reject the conclusion of the argument in the *Republic* holding that God, being perfect, cannot change. On what grounds is this rejection

made? It is not enough to point to the contradiction in combining the conclusion of
the argument with the contingency of the
world and the divine knowledge of that
world. It must be shown directly that the
platonic argument is invalid.

Kant suggested a possible objection to
the very idea of unincreasable perfection
but characteristically drew from the objection not the need to revise the idea, but
rather only the need to renounce claims of
supporting the idea by theoretical reason.[2]
It was Whitehead who first clearly stated
the Kantian objection as ground for a revised definition of divine excellence. The
objection is that there are incompossible
values so that the notion of all possible
value, fully actualized, is contradictory.[3]
Leibniz had acknowledged that the ontological argument presupposes what can be
challenged, the belief that the definition
of deity as the "sum of possible perfections" makes consistent sense. Leibniz
argued, however, that there can be contradiction only between positive and negative predicates, and perfections are wholly

positive. But in truth (as Kant points out) there can be contradiction between equally positive predicates. Thus "red here now" contradicts "green here now." Or, if a poet chooses to express a certain sentiment in a sonnet rather than in some other verse form, what is rejected in such choice is as positive as what is affirmed. The whole point of contingency lies here, that actualization, decision, is always exclusive of positive values. Only fanatics think there is a uniquely good solution to every problem. Even God must make contingent decisions to create a world; he must rule out *good* alternatives. Even he cannot have the values of all possible worlds, all fully actualized. According to Whitehead, this is the rationale for becoming, that no actuality can leave nothing further to seek. Divine potentiality for value is absolutely infinite, but not even divine actuality can ever exhaustively actualize this potentiality. Spinoza's proof for his necessitarianism can be shown to depend upon the assumption that perfection, in the sense of exhaustive actualization of the possible, is itself possible. For one who denies this possibility, the proof, like that of Leibniz for the possibility of unincreasable perfection, has no force. Process philosophy makes the denial, not skeptically or agnostically as does Kant, but categorically. Hence process philosophy revises the definition of divine excellence. My way of putting this revision is to say that God is ideally good and great, not by being an absolute and unincreasable maximum of value, but by being *unsurpassable by another* than himself. As Fechner brilliantly put it a century ago, only God can surpass God, but this he perpetually does by ideally absorbing the riches of creation into himself.

The other unfinished business in our express trip through history is what happens to the idea of "matter," which was so important in Greek and medieval thought. For some philosophers "matter" is the name for an answer to a certain question. For others, of whom Leibniz was the first Western representative, it is merely a name for the question itself, not an answer. The question is, in the change from one

state of things to another, what, other than
form, i.e., definite qualities or properties
(essential or accidental to the things), survives through the change? Aristotle said,
the "matter" survives, and this, with the
essential forms, constitutes the identity of
the things or substances. The trouble is, if
we abstract from all definite form, nothing
definite seems to be left. What is this, in
itself wholly indefinite, something called
matter? Aristotle (and I think Aquinas)
admitted that matter as such is known
only by analogy. However, the analogy is
with something itself quite problematic.
Thus, if clay is modeled into a statue, the
clay is matter compared to the shape given
it in the statue. But what after all is clay?
We know it in terms of its form, and modern physics finds nothing specifiable as
persistent through physical changes except certain forms expressable mathemati-
cally as certain relational patterns. To say
that the same matter persists through the
succession of forms seems to add nothing
but words to our knowledge. A hydrogen
molecule is such by virtue of its form, and

the persistence of the molecule is known solely as the persistence of the form.

There is another difficulty. As Descartes said (and Augustine had said it before him), physical reality is essentially spatial or extended. Extension, as Leibniz saw, is a matter of relations. It is complex, not a simple quality like redness. Thus a circle has its parts in a different set of relations from a square. Location in space is relative, a matter of being nearer, that is causally more immediately effective upon and affected by, some things than others. Extension is thus not an ultimate, further unanalyzable idea but coincides with a certain form of relatedness. In relativity physics an account is given of the essential difference between spatial relations and temporal ones. The difference is that between one-way causal dependencies, later upon earlier, not vice versa, and two-way relations, either of mutual independence (of single events) or mutual interaction (of things, i.e., event sequences, open to mutual influence with the speed of light). None of this tells us what sorts of things or events are able to have these relations. "Matter" or "physical" reality is merely a label for whatever can have them, it is not an answer to the question, what sorts of things can do so? The Democritean theory of matter told the story right at the beginning: an atom is a bit of "being" in "non-being," i.e., in mere space, the void. Matter is not a special kind of being save insofar as its shape or other forms are special. Matter is only something or other, as opposed to nothing.

Traditionally there were other factors. Thus matter was potentiality in contrast to actuality, potential form in contrast to actual form. Also matter was insentient. In combination with the first point, the second makes sense only on the supposition that mind as such is purely actual, so that something else is needed to constitute potentiality. To some of us this seems a very odd idea of mind, with its sense of past and future, the former as already definite and beyond influence, the latter as in principle partly indeterminate but determinable and even now in process of being further determined. What is potentiality but this determinable indeterminacy of the future? What is mind apart from the process of experiencing the already determined past and evaluating and deciding options for the future? Mind is activity, thinking, feeling, remembering, planning, deciding—and this activity is in principle both actuality and possibility. Does it really help to illuminate experiencing to suppose bits of mere stuff, or mere somethings, persisting through it?

However, common sense and many philosophers point to what seems good evidence that insentient somethings exist. Concerning this evidence Leibniz, with a stroke of high genius, made the following little understood suggestion: there are indeed insentient things, e.g., rocks, gases, liquids, the earth; but these are aggregates of invisibly minute entities *to which the criteria for absolute insentience do not apply.* These criteria are *inertness* (and even at absolute zero atoms are not entirely inert) plus lack of unity. Maxwell later compared a gas to a swarm of bees. The swarm may seem immobile, or to move slowly in a languid way, but the individual bees are highly active, and each bee moves as one, not as a mere aggregate. The dynamism of a gas is in the atoms or molecules. So, according to Leibniz, is the sentience. It comes to this, the dichotomy sentient-insentient is not a qualitative contrast, but a *difference of logical type*, that between the singular and the aggregate. In my opinion this is the real secret of the concept of "merely physical" reality. When we don't know the dynamism we seem to face an inert mass, or one lacking in definite unities (thus a wind).

There is still the question: What persists, other than form, from past to present? Answer, what persists is *the past itself,* so far as it is still present in memory and perception. The poet Longfellow almost stated the process philosophy point when he wrote, "All are architects of fate . . . our todays and yesterdays are the bricks with which we build." The past as still grasped (mostly unconsciously, or without introspective awareness) in the present is the "stuff" we have from the past. Human perception as well as memory, according to Whitehead, is intuition of the past, especially, so far as perception is concerned, of immediately past events within the body, above all in the nervous system, but also, slightly indirectly, of events in the near environment outside the body. Perception is (in my phrase) impersonal "memory" (in the broad sense—intuition of past processes); and what we ordinarily call by the word is personal, giving us our own past human experiences. Thus mind as both sense of the past and intending, partly deciding, the future covers all the functions of matter. I have yet to learn of any such function it cannot perform, provided one is sufficiently imaginative (as many are not), in conceiving the possible varieties of mind other than human, or even animal, with aspects of thought and consciousness reduced almost to zero in some cases. Leibniz was a great innovator in all this.

Leibniz made two major and interrelated mistakes in his theory of matter. One was that he took the genetic identity of a substance or monad to be absolute, a strict law of succession, thus excluding both creative moment by moment decision and also interactions between monads. The other was that he admitted memory as intuition of the personal past but not perception in the proper sense of intuition of the impersonal past, the past of other individuals. The monad "mirrors" the other monads, but only via the preestablished harmony, which is not a direct givenness of other singulars, but a mere correspondence, which God alone knows intuitively (by a principle not accounted for in the system). The famous doctrine of "windowless monads" radically distorts the impersonal aspect of experiencing, i.e., perception. Peirce and Whitehead, students of Leibniz, remedy this defect, as they do certain other bizarre features of the monadology.

For theology the revised Leibnizian theory has a certain importance. It means that whereas traditional theology other than Berkeleyan had to relate God to two sorts of entities, minds and mere bodies, process theology needs to consider only the first. Moreover, the relation is intelligible by the very principle that explains the relations of memory and perception to their data in created minds. We are influenced by the personal and impersonal past because we intuit them. We are influenced by God because we intuit God. (Even Aquinas admits such an intuition, or, as a French writer terms it, *"la saisie immédiate de dieu."*) In process philosophy we, or the created minds, influence God for the same reason, that is, God intuits, or, in Whitehead's phrase, "prehends" them. The single principle of prehending, which is but an aspect of "creativity" or experience as, in principle and always, partly active or self-creative, utilizing previous events as materials for new syntheses, the syntheses themselves furnishing new such materials, and so on forever—this principle expresses not only how the world hangs together, but also how it depends upon and yet also influences God. No more magnificent metaphysical generalization has ever been made.

Gilson, when at Harvard with Whitehead, complained that he could not understand "creativity." "Is it a substance? Is it an attribute?" I respond, fifty years later, with the analogous queries: What, in Thomism, is "being"? Is it a substance, or an attribute? What is the "act of existing"? Whitehead's theory of creativity is his attempt to communicate his "intuition" (he uses that word here) of the act of existing. That this is not a single substance or a mere attribute seems clear. It is not God, because each creature exists by its *own* act of existing, dependent to be sure upon antecedent acts, including the antecedent eminent actions of deity. But finally each actuality exists by its own self-activity: it is creative, however trivially, of new determinateness, thereby enriching reality as previously there, including divine reality as previously there.

Berdyaev, Whitehead, and Tillich, three prominent and in many ways very different writers concerned with philosophy of religion, agree, almost in so many words, that the creatures, by their partly free or self-determining acts "enrich the divine life itself." In this doctrine they give a new meaning to the old saying, "the end of all existence is the glory of God." For my religious sense this consideration alone would lead me to prefer the new idea of perfection as capable of increase to the old idea of an immutable or absolute maximum. (Also the avoidance of the classical problem of evil made possible by the new philosophy would seem almost enough to justify the same preference.) Very literally we exist to enhance, not simply to admire or enjoy, the divine glory. Ultimately we are contributors to the ever-growing divine treasury of values. We serve God, God is not finally means to our ends. Our final and inclusive end is to contribute to the divine life.

If this view seems to make God lacking in generosity, I suggest that the all-knowing and all-loving cannot give happiness to others without fully participating in and possessing this happiness just because it is

realized by the others. For such is love at
its fullest, joy in the joy, and sorrow in the
sorrow, of others. The injunction, "seek to
further a good beyond your own," applies
only to creatures that die and are more or
less incapable of appreciating the benefits
they may bestow upon others. The imperishable and all-appreciating Eminent Being, however, can act for the good of all
without transcending his own good as the
inclusive goal. Thomists will perhaps see
that there is in this something analogous
to certain doctrines of the Angelic Doctor—
analogous to, but clearly not identical
with, those doctrines. Such is the "anti-
Thomistic Thomism" of one exponent and
explorer of the new possibilities that this
century has discovered for philosophical
or natural theology.

Gilson once wrote that we should all
make our choice between Aquinas and
Kant. He fails to show and could not show
that these two thinkers exhaust the reasonable possibilities. They both share a
concept of substance which the Buddhists
had criticized effectively over a thousand

years before. They both define God in essentially the same way, by analogy, but
with the requirement that there be no
possibility of change, no unactualized but
actualizable potentiality, in his reality. Of
course, there must be analogical aspects
in the idea, but is it analogy to turn things
upside down, as one must do to have as
what corresponds to knowing in God the
very opposite of what it is in creatures?
Neither Thomism nor Kantianism has any
clear idea of creativity as a "transcenden-
tal," applicable to every creature and also
to the creator. Both take too literally the
idea of "sufficient" causal condition, or
the strongest form of the principle of sufficient reason. Events have necessary conditions and conditions "sufficient" for their
possibility. But what suffices for present
actuality is only the new act of existing
inherent in the present effect and not there
in any past or eternal cause at all.

The objection to the notion of creative
causation, meaning that which produces a
net increase in reality, was that the cause
"cannot give what it lacks"! As though

temporal genesis were a mere passing out,
or passing on, of something already real!
Rather it is growth, passage from less to
more, in short, creation. The effect is not
"given," it does not "come from" some
antecedent haven, it becomes (German *es
wird*), and this idea is ultimate. No jug-
gling with "being and not being" will turn
the two into becoming. Rather, starting
with becoming, we can abstract being and
not-being as aspects. The past is, the future is not, except in the form of a range
of possibilities, some more probable than
others, out of which there *will be* some
definite determination and exclusion, although there is no wholly definite determination of which one can truly say in
advance that it will be.

Medieval theology and Kantianism
share certain elements that I call material-
istic. The old comparison of deity with the
sun, giving off energy while neither losing
nor gaining any itself, was a metaphor the
basis of which was not only physical rather
than spiritual but was in fact mythical,
since there neither is nor could be such a

physical object. Far too little use was
made of our higher levels of experience,
love, sympathy, perception, memory, in
thinking analogically about deity. In
Kant's case there is a special form of ma-
terialism in the reasoning about *substance*.
Kant says that change implies a something
that remains identical through change,
and he rejects a psychical theory of this
something on the ground that the "soul"
is too variable to meet the requirements.
So he opts for the physical atoms (or point-
forces) as the (phenomenal) substance.
But change is no ultimate, not further
analyzable idea, since it can be explained
as the becoming of novelty in successive
steps. We say that the weather changes,
but the fact can be expressed by report-
ing successive contrasting temperatures,
etc. If in present experience there is memory of previous joy or sorrow, succeeded
by sorrow or joy, certainly there has been
change, i.e., the becoming of novel actuality. As for identity, as we have seen, the
past itself is intuited; also there are always
some common characters between succes-

sive experiences, and in personal memory there is normally a special intimacy and congruence between earlier and later.

Kant's idea of the summum bonum is largely medieval, a posthumous career (outside of time? In time? The mind boggles at Kant's doctrine here.). In this posthumous state, thanks to divine control, happiness and goodness will, or may, approach perfect correspondence. God is the means to this desired end, not the end itself. A wholly immutable deity can only be a means in relation to creaturely purposes. This is obscured by language tending to gloss over the issue, as when God is declared the good for every creature. The trouble is that our enjoyment of this good is no contribution to the divine good itself, which is defined as entirely self-sufficient. Some of us seek a God we can serve, as much as or more than a God who can serve us. Indeed the final function of God is to "endow our fleeting days with abiding significance" (Jewish ritual) by enabling our actions to enrich the divine life, which is imperishable and incorruptible (two dicta of the negative theology that need no qualifications or apologies).

I have quarreled enough with Gilson, a scholar from whom I have learned quite a little. I will now quarrel with Sir Karl Popper, from whom I have learned more, and whom I put high in the list of living philosophers. He attacks Whitehead's metaphysics by singling out a passage, rather unusual for Whitehead, in which rhetorical vividness is more apparent than precision.[4] This is the notorious series of paradoxes about God and the world creating each other, and the like. Sir Karl says he tried to be fair in choosing the selection. He could have been more fair had he chosen another passage, or rather two passages, which in combination have the same purpose, but express it with more care, the passages in which Whitehead formally characterizes the two aspects, primordial and consequent, of deity. The point, which Popper says he does not understand, is Whitehead's version of dual transcendence. Popper presumably has not had occasion to look very far into the history of this idea, except perhaps in the to me unsatisfactory form that it takes in Hegel.

One side of God's nature is said to be "infinite, free, complete, primordial, eternal, actually deficient, and unconscious." The other side is "determined, incomplete, consequent, everlasting [meaning incorruptible, all change being gain, not loss], fully actual, and conscious." The primordial nature is conceptual, "limited by no actuality which it presupposes," whereas the consequent nature "originates with physical experience derived from the temporal world and then acquires integration with the primordial side." It is clear that for Whitehead God is both infinite and finite ("it belongs to the nature of physical experience that it is finite"). It should be said here that "physical" in Whitehead merely means experience whose data are concrete and particular, rather than abstract or general. Infinity in the absolute sense is a conceptual entity, concerned with possibilities as such; not a possible actuality. It is also clear that while the primordial nature is eternally complete and hence immutable, the consequent nature is subject to novelty in the form of additions, but not of loss or decrease. Thus Whitehead is in the tradition begun by Socinus, continued in a long line of mostly little known writers, few of whom, it seems, were read by him or his critics. This is one of the many reasons why so many have had difficulty reading him. It is also one reason why I had less trouble than most. I was already in this tradition. I believed that there was novelty in God's knowledge and that this did not imply any defect in that knowledge. Eventually I encountered the Socinian argument for this view.

Popper once wrote me that my having known Whitehead was an important reason why I see more in him than he, Popper, can. I am not sure about the importance of this factor. None of my Harvard, Freiburg, or Marburg teachers influenced me as Peirce, whom I have never seen, did. I could give many other examples. Books have been the great events in my life, apart from a few friends other than philosophers.

In an article on "Theism" that is in some respects very able in the *Encyclopaedia of Philosophy* edited by Paul Edwards, a brief account of Whitehead's theology ends with the observation that the "admitted and severe paradoxes" of the position make it doubtful if this approach can supersede the classical one. I note that the paradoxes are not spelled out, and what is more significant some of the paradoxes that have led so many to reject classical theism (the doctrine of simple transcendence, God as the immutable absolute) are also not spelled out, and some of them are not even mentioned. This is the way philosophical controversy often, though fortunately not always, tends to go. Sometimes present insights are dismissed in favor of tradition, sometimes a new fashion is exalted above any need for assimilating the past. Example of the latter: Wittgenstein.

I have tried to show that the development of ideas during the last seven centuries of speculative thought about theism has a certain sense and has enlarged our comprehension substantially. This is part of the answer to Popper's complaint that when Whitehead appeals to progress as the justification of the speculative effort he fails to follow through and exhibit that progress. In Whitehead's work as a whole I think he did contribute effectively to such an exhibition. To me it is really evident that Whitehead's thinking took the basic insights of Spinoza, Leibniz, and Hume into account in a way that those three thinkers could not have taken process philosophy's insights into account. There is an asymmetry in the growth of philosophic ideas that is less different from that in the growth of scientific ones than is always realized. Spinoza, Leibniz, or Hume could learn from process philosophy things they did not clearly conceive at all, whereas what they could teach a mature process philosopher is little more than the latter already knows—in part by studying these very predecessors. "Philosophy never entirely recovers from the shock of a great philosopher" was Whitehead's way of putting this asymmetry. We do—or can —stand on the shoulders of the great men of the past.

NOTES

1. For a translation of this Fechnerian passage see *Philosophers Speak of God*, by Hartshorne and Reese (The University of Chicago Press, 1953, 1963), p. 252. In this book documentation for many of the historical points made in this Aquinas Lecture may be found.

2. See Kant's essay, *Ein Versuch die negative Grösse in die Weltweisheit einzuführen.*

3. On incompossible values see Hartshorne and Reese, *op. cit.*, pp. v, 10, 279 (384), 284, 287, 506.

4. See Karl Popper, *The Open Society and Its Enemies* (Princeton: Princeton University Press, 1966), pp. 247-250.

The Aquinas Lectures

Published by the Marquette University Press
Milwaukee, Wisconsin 53233

St. Thomas and the Life of Learning (1937) by
John F. McCormick, S.J., (1874-1943) professor of philosophy, Loyola University.

sbn 87462-101-1

St. Thomas and the Gentiles (1938) by Mortimer J. Adler, Ph.D., director of the Institute of Philosophical Research, San Francisco, Calif.

sbn 87462-102-X

St. Thomas and the Greeks (1939) by Anton C. Pegis, Ph.D., professor of philosophy, Pontifical Institute of Mediaeval Studies, Toronto.

sbn 87462-103-8

The Nature and Functions of Authority (1940) by Yves Simon, Ph.D., (1903-1961) professor of philosophy of social thought, University of Chicago.

sbn 87462-104-6

St. Thomas and Analogy (1941) by Gerald B. Phelan, Ph.D., (1892-1965) professor of philosophy, St. Michael's College, Toronto.

sbn 87462-105-4

St. Thomas and the Problem of Evil (1942) by Jacques Maritain, Ph.D., professor *emeritus* of philosophy, Princeton University.

sbn 87462-106-2

Humanism and Theology (1943) by Werner Jaeger, Ph.D., Litt.D., (1888-1961) University professor, Harvard University. SBN 87462-107-0

The Nature and Origins of Scientism (1944) by John Wellmuth. SBN 87462-108-9

Cicero in the Courtroom of St. Thomas Aquinas (1945) by E. K. Rand, Ph.D., Litt.D., LL.D., (1871-1945) Pope professor of Latin, *emeritus,* Harvard University. SBN 87462-109-7

St. Thomas and Epistemology (1946) by Louis-Marie Regis, O.P., Th.L., Ph.D., director of the Albert the Great Institute of Mediaeval Studies, University of Montreal.
SBN 87462-110-0

St. Thomas and the Greek Moralists (1947, Spring) by Vernon J. Bourke, Ph.D., professor of philosophy, St. Louis University, St. Louis, Missouri. SBN 87462-111-9

History of Philosophy and Philosophical Education (1947, Fall) by Etienne Gilson of the *Académie française,* director of studies and professor of the history of Mediaeval philosophy, Pontifical Institute of Mediaeval Studies, Toronto. SBN 87462-112-7

The Natural Desire for God (1948) by William R. O'Connor, S.T.L., Ph.D., former professor of dogmatic theology, St. Joseph's Seminary, Dunwoodie, N.Y. SBN 87462-113-5

St. Thomas and the World State (1949) by Robert M. Hutchins, former Chancellor of the University of Chicago, president of the Fund for the Republic. SBN 87462-114-3

Method in Metaphysics (1950) by Robert J. Henle, S.J., Ph.D., academic vice-president, St. Louis University, St. Louis, Missouri.
SBN 87462-115-1

Wisdom and Love in St. Thomas Aquinas (1951) by Étienne Gilson of the *Académie française,* director of studies and professor of the history of Mediaeval philosophy, Pontifical Institute of Mediaeval Studies, Toronto.
SBN 87462-116-X

The Good in Existential Metaphysics (1952) by Elizabeth G. Salmon, Ph.D., professor of philosophy in the graduate school, Fordham University. SBN 87462-117-8

St. Thomas and the Object of Geometry (1953) by Vincent Edward Smith, Ph.D., director, Philosophy of Science Institute, St. John's University. SBN 87462-118-6

Realism and Nominalism Revisited (1954) by Henry Veatch, Ph.D., professor and chairman of the department of philosophy, Northwestern University. SBN 87462-119-4

Imprudence in St. Thomas Aquinas (1955) by Charles J. O'Neil, Ph.D., professor of philosophy, Villanova University. SBN 87462-120-8

The Truth That Frees (1956) by Gerard Smith, S.J., Ph.D., professor of philosophy, Marquette University. sBN 87462-121-6

St. Thomas and the Future of Metaphysics (1957) by Joseph Owens, C.Ss.R., Ph.D., professor of philosophy, Pontifical Institute of Mediaeval Studies, Toronto. sBN 87462-122-4

Thomas and the Physics of 1958: A Confrontation (1958) by Henry Margenau, Ph.D., Eugene Higgins professor of physics and natural philosophy, Yale University.
sBN 87462-123-2

Metaphysics and Ideology (1959) by Wm. Oliver Martin, Ph.D., professor of philosophy, University of Rhode Island. sBN 87462-124-0

Language, Truth and Poetry (1960) by Victor M. Hamm, Ph.D., professor of English, Marquette University. sBN 87462-125-9

Metaphysics and Historicity (1961) by Emil L. Fackenheim, Ph.D., professor of philosophy, University of Toronto. sBN 87462-126-7

The Lure of Wisdom (1962) by James D. Collins, Ph.D., professor of philosophy, St. Louis University. sBN 87462-127-5

Religion and Art (1963) by Paul Weiss, Ph.D. Sterling professor of philosophy, Yale University. sBN 87462-128-3

St. Thomas and Philosophy (1964) by Anton C. Pegis, Ph.D., professor of philosophy, Pontifical Institute of Mediaeval Studies, Toronto.
SBN 87462-129-1

The University In Process (1965) by John O. Riedl, Ph.D., dean of faculty, Queensboro Community College. SBN 87462-130-5

The Pragmatic Meaning of God (1966) by Robert O. Johann, associate professor of philosophy, Fordham University.
SBN 87462-131-3

Religion and Empiricism (1967) by John E. Smith, Ph.D., professor of philosophy, Yale University. SBN 87462-132-1

The Subject (1968) by Bernard Lonergan, S.J., S.T.D., professor of Dogmatic Theory, Regis College, Ontario and Gregorian University, Rome. SBN 87462-133-X

Beyond Trinity (1969) by Bernard J. Cooke, S.T.D. SBN 87462-134-8

Ideas and Concepts (1970) by Julius R. Weinberg, Ph.D., (1908-1971) Vilas Professor of Philosophy, University of Wisconsin.
SBN 87462-135-6

Reason and Faith Revisited (1971) by Francis H. Parker, Ph.D., head of the philosophy department, Purdue University, Lafayette, Indiana. SBN 87462-136-4

Psyche and Cerebrum (1972) by John N. Findlay, M.A. Oxon., Ph.D., Clark Professor of Moral Philosophy and Metaphysics, Yale University.
ISBN 0-87462-137-2

The Problem of the Criterion (1973) by Roderick M. Chisholm, Ph.D., Andrew W. Mellon Professor in the Humanities, Brown University.
ISBN 0-87462-138-0

Man as Infinite Spirit (1974) by James H. Robb, Ph.D., professor of philosophy, Marquette University.
ISBN 0-87462-139-9

The Beginning and the Beyond (1975) by Eric Voegelin, Ph.D. In preparation.

Aquinas to Whitehead: Seven Centuries of Metaphysics of Religion (1976) by Charles E. Hartshorne, Ph.D., professor of philosophy, the University of Texas at Austin.
ISBN 0-87462-141-0

Uniform format, cover and binding.